Thousands Flee
California Wildflowers
SCOT SIEGEL

salmonpoetry

Published in 2012 by
Salmon Poetry
Cliffs of Moher, County Clare, Ireland
Website: www.salmonpoetry.com
Email: info@salmonpoetry.com

ISBN 978-1-907056-94-9

COVER ARTWORK: *"Evolution of Behavior Theory" by Randy Richmond*
COVER DESIGN: *Siobhán Hutson*

For Debbie

Acknowledgements

I wish to thank the editors and readers of the following publications where poems from this collection, some in earlier versions, first appeared:

Aesthetica, Alba, American Poetry Journal, A-Minor, Dark Sky Magazine, Drash, Front Porch Journal, High Desert Journal, MiPOesias, Naugatuck River Review, New Verse News, OCHO, Oregon Stories, Poemeleon, Poets/Artists, Press 1, The Externalist, The Oregonian, Right Hand Pointing, Referential Magazine, San Pedro River Review, Short, Fast and Deadly, Stirring, Thunderclap Magazine, Touch: the journal of healing, Thrush, Verseweavers.

"Reasons I Resisted Kissing Your Sister," first published by *MiPOesias*, was a finalist for Aesthetica Magazine's Creative Works Contest and is anthologized in *Aesthetica Creative Works Annual* 2011. "Lucky Star," first published in *Drash: Northwest Mosaic* (Volume III), is anthologized in *Before We Have Nowhere to Stand* (Lost Horse Press, 2012). "Fire Poker," first published in *Front Porch Journal*, Texas State University MFA Program, 2010, is anthologized in *Dogs Singing: A Tribute Anthology*, Salmon Poetry, 2011.

Poets/Artists nominated "Placer County Roadside Marker" for a Pushcart Prize in 2011.

New Verse News nominated "Autumn Turns Through Stratified Wars" for a Pushcart Prize in 2009.

Referential Magazine nominated "Farallones" ("Gulls in the Absence of Stars) for Sundress Publications' *Best of the Net* in 2010.

Naugatuck River Review nominated "Somewhere, Under the Rainbow" for a Puschart Prize in 2011.

OCHO nominated "Mochi Salvation" for a Pushcart Prize in 2011.

Some poems from this collection first appeared in the chapbooks: *Untitled Country*, Pudding House Publications, 2009; and *Skeleton Says*, Finishing Line Press, 2010.

An audio recording of "Heaven of the Moment," first published by Press 1, is featured online at *Whale Sound*. An audio recording of "A Little Sweetness at Café Marzocca," read by Didi Menendez, and recordings of "Don't Ask, Don't Tell" and "Drawbridge," read by the author, are published online at *MiPOesias/MiPO Radio*.

I wish to thank Maureen Alsop, Paul Watsky, and John Morrison for reading earlier drafts of some poems; Jessie Lendennie of Salmon Poetry for selecting and editing the manuscript; Siobhán Hutson of Salmon Poetry for designing the book; and my family for understanding and supporting me in this solitary work of poetry. I have my daughter Caroline to thank for the title.

Contents

I. After The Summer of Love

II. At Home In The World

III. Song of the California Wildfire

IV. Drawbridge

I. After The Summer of Love

> *"We have to deal with where we are.*
> *We have to create cooperatives; we have to create*
> *intentional communities; we have to work*
> *for local cooperation where we are."*
>
> JERRY BROWN, Governor of California
> (1975-1983; 2011–present)

Reasons I Resisted Kissing Your Sister

Do you remember the Playboys we cached in the hollowed-out eucalyptus? I never found them again. How about that night cat-fishing at the quarry below Payless, when that monster locked its jaws on your wrist and began to swim; I thought of Persephone then.

And do you remember getting lost in a storm sewer, the roar of Oakland Avenue above our heads. Then a pinpoint of light through a catch basin that was welded shut; I was tempted to kiss her then.

But later that summer at camp without you I walked with a girl from the East, high on a desert trail, our hands clasped beside the Tawanamas, mountains bristling before a storm. For a moment,

I thought of you and your mother back in the city. I was hoping you were sober. I almost thought of your sister. But the girl's fist warm in my palm, juniper smoke in her green eyes, and the blue sky turning purple in the distance…

Do you remember the grassfire we set on the hill above your house? That was the last time you told me your sister wanted to kiss me. But her chest was flat as the valley, and her face freckled and pale as the oat grass. She looked like you brother, and I thought you knew better.

Geraniums

In the beginning
Cronkite whispered

through the walls
of my mother's sternum

I am not a Baby Boomer
too young for Vietnam

Though I saw Bobby shot
saw his head roll back

and the light grow dim
on an 8-inch

black and white Sony...

~

Faint recollection
The Summer of Love

Dance of the neighbor girl
with one leg on a hook

and a ghoulish smile—
I was just an infant

Though I remember the stink
of geraniums

when the news came on
and the world went dark

in my mother's eyes.

Chris, 1975

We were best friends
He gave me brass medals

pulled from the coat
in his mother's closet

He taught me to roll a smoke
like a stoic private

We huddled in the side yard
by the chrysanthemums; cupped

our hands, held a flame
out of the wind

just under the chimney
cleanout…

Summer nights we flicked
butane Bics

torched little army men
whirled them about

We scorched each other's
wrists and arms and thighs…

We laughed madly
in pretend tents, lighters

illuminating
nylon sleeping bags—

Chris had blond hair
and blue eyes

Nimble on the tennis court
Chris was well versed

in the strategies of chess
and Vietcong tactics

Chris had an affinity for
Hitler. I didn't

understand this: Chris,
whose father had

never come home.

Trajectory

after AC & AW

It has been years and I still smell bay laurels
burning in the park, still see you drifting the aisles
of a minimart, lugging your case of brew. It's been
thirty years since you rode off. I still struggle

The difficulty is like deciphering the scent
of late-summer jasmine, or raspberry Jell-O
with vodka shots, or sensimilla smoke curling
from the bong water. I want to say

I was wrong. But your names always began
with 'Y'. Now I see you speeding down Oakland
Avenue, like black windflowers through a hedgerow.
The cops are on you with blue and red lasers—

Y number one: You were the drummer!
Oh, how you admired your brother, three years
your senior and the lead guitarist in a garage
band called "Detour"

And Y number two: Our leading rusher!
We cheered for you until our lungs cramped
Then no one was there for the final snap, the hand-
off from black leather seat to slick asphalt…

Had I been there, I would have kissed you
and consoled your hysterical sisters. I would have
kissed them too, and steered you away from the bike
Before your last breathless flight into winter.

A Little Sweetness at Café Marzocca

The barista's going on about a little girl
with red curls and hundred-dollar jeans
who reaches into the tip jar

The barista sees her, and it's a standoff,
a seesaw staring match in the middle
of the midday rush

The barista wants to tell her mother,
but the sun slants through the blinds
and she's lost in a dream,

recounting her own childhood—
The toy she wanted badly but didn't get;
the gift that went to her sister—

Then mother enters and they face
one another, and the girl has the gall
to ask for *a piece of candy!*

But she's so charming, flashing two
one-dollar bills, like revolvers,
in the barista's face—

And we see the anguish rise
in the young woman's eyes, dark eyes
that say, *I'm doing my best, but she's killing me!*

And the barista wants nothing more
than to see the bad girl squirm;
Watch mother dress her down,

Teach her a lesson she'll never forget;
the one she'll spend the rest of her life
reliving.

Don't Ask, Don't Tell

*"About 280,000 vehicles cross the Bay Bridge daily,
some as 'casual carpools' – a form of organized hitchhiking
whereby drivers pick up strangers on their way to work."*

Via, Newsletter of American Automobile Association

It's all gray at the bridge toll backup. Winter
Always winter here and raining hard
when it's your turn to drive

Your new rideshare companion curls up like a cat
in the heated leather seat beside you. Asian,
though French you guess from her purr

Twenty, maybe twenty-four. You found her
on Craigslist. You know nothing about her
and of course she knows nothing of you

She's comfortable enough in your escort—
slowly nodding off—But when you reach down
for the stick, she grips the leather strap of her

Black workbag a little harder, as if rendered
by an early morning dream that has returned
and taken hold

You turn up the heat and she breathes uneasily,
shifts in her seat. Though as her flushed cheek
turns, she smiles like daybreak, her breath

Tinctured with sage, raspberry, warm Belgian
chocolate—Doesn't matter that you could be her
mother. Doesn't matter if you are a woman

or a man. The distance between you is con-
founding—You don't know if you can trust your
self with the truth.

Autumn Turns Through Stratified Wars

A few little leaves alight on the sleeper wind
lemon, iron-orange, vermilion
but there's no dive-swiping gnat-catching tonight

Songbirds sense the slack-season upon us
stillness readies the river, trees glimmer
and we lean uneasily into the quiet...

Three warblers balance on one blackberry cane
not ordinary warblers, yellow-breasted chats
gone silent in the breeze—

There's no yellow chip; no whistle, caw, nor rattle
just three imperceptible heartbeats screaming
through silver thorns & bramble—

Is their night not unlike our country?
Somewhere, a raptor hovers, drags her talons
over Arab neighborhoods, while we lie awake...

In my wife's eyes a blue flame flickers
World News, a helicopter turns, delivering
or receiving the dead...

We hardly notice midnight passing over
as we tilt and spin on the dreadful wing of a hawk
Who says she loves us?

Crows on our tail, relentless—
I think I hear one say:

Come home.

Words for the Wedding Rehearsal Dinner

for John and Jill

They say, every seven years
the body renews itself:

one by one, every cell's
replaced, until your

childhood, a shadow
in the foreground,

looks on, unrecognizable
even to itself—

That's why a moment
is a miracle—

Bay winds have ceased,
bees drunk on blue hyacinths

have fallen to the ground,
their tiny wings arrested,

and every cell in you
stands still, aglow,

and we can tell

II. At Home In The World

"A people free to choose will always choose peace."
RONALD REAGAN

Lucky Star

Before the State of Israel
in the country of everlasting night

They became dust before they died
for a country of light, before it was...

They had no flag
      no song
      no homeland...

But an indigo shield arched over them,
and now us, like a prayer,

With a yellow star
emblazoned upon it.

Untitled Country

There is an odd country, beyond Democracy,
where few live, though many look in
and ask about visas. They say, that country
has no borders

Their flag, the color of wind, never flies at
half-staff; their national anthem, called
conversation, changes daily
depending on the weather—

That country has no army
Its citizens, even the littlest children,
are allowed to vote; and their votes
count twice.

Did I mention, in that country
they celebrate Independence Day
every twenty-four hours,
even in the dead of winter.

Idling, Sacramento

Standing at the edge of this country
of ghost trains and swallowed rivers,
I can look into the face of any traveler
and tell who is at home in the world.

It is not in the style of dress, or the mess
in the back of the car. It is not in the race
of an idle, or the wear on the treads for
having traveled so far.

It is in the way they wait, some way back
from the line, while others nose forward
tempting the light. It is in the way they
acknowledge me, a veteran in need of a job—

Some nod, a few salute—
But mostly they quickly turn away.

New Year's Revelers at the End of a Decade

They do not want to be the last ones to leave
looking like they have no place to go—

The road from here to there is long
and shadowy; three orphan wars

mark the distances they've travelled
in our country's lock-step sleep...

A whole generation of American
children have grown up

in a foreign country,
he tells her—

Though she does not listen. She does not
answer... Rather, she gestures

to the oak in a dialect of snowy
allegiance, the giant oak on their street

that held the sun in its arms
like a baby last summer

Song of the Hospice Provider

Leah leans over a warm porcelain basin
rinses stiff maple syrup from a crystal dish

Winter sun strikes one side of her drawn face
in variegated shafts through the dusty panes

For years, she helped him remember himself
rearranged trophies on the shelf in his study

She'd touch his wrist at the right time of day
& pour warm tea for the two of them

But he became steam rising from the rim of a
chipped cup; a low fog lifting

from a reed-lined pond, caught in the lee
of a low grassy hill

scuttled by the sun—

Visiting the Masons' Grand Lodge

The glass is half-empty. The night fills it with sighs
We came for a good time, my wife and I—
kids at summer camp—Even after twenty years,
some things we still do on a whim…

It's late. Packing now. Didn't even stay the night
The lodge and its rooms are dingy & warn
with the pall of those who lived and died here
(a siren wails from the highway below)

Ten years ago the last resident left in protest
The Grand is boutique hotel now. Micro beers and
a movie house. Tourists and young executives
drink without a designated driver. Play truth or dare,
watch foreign films, or screw, for a change…

Our room is hot and it smells like the old, she says
Though I think hospital… poor farm… asylum…
I wonder how many died right here in this room
where the walls feel dank, the sash window sticks

and the radiator sits, silent as a minister,
(no hiss… no spit) idle as a visitor
slouched in the corner, when I turn
and close the door behind us.

Somewhere, Under the Rainbow

I've never driven off with the fuel nozzle attached; though I saw it
happen once: 'twas a swelterin' Indian summer day in Pomona.
She was eatin' a burger while barkin' orders at a gaggle of soccer
players in the back of a red minivan. It shimmied as she pulled away
and that black rubber snake became a cartoon neck stretched

beyond belief before it snapped and whipped like an unmanned
fire hose; and she kept on drivin', juggling fries, cell phone
slippin' from her cheek, fallin' between a greasy bucket
seat and muddy center console.

Sure I could've chased her down, but I was late for a drink
so I paused and gawked with the other Disney characters
as the gusher doused the dumbfounded attendant, who slumped
against the air pump like a clubfoot mushroom while his partner
emerged from the minimart restroom smokin'!

The scene bloomed like a psilocybin rainbow; so before I could
become fully sated by the fumes, I pulled a quick U-ee
and punched it in the opposite direction....

I can still see her fussin' with the belt, eyes bulgin' like a smelt
with the bends, as she reached for a lever that wasn't there, maybe
thinkin' she'd left the emergency brake on and that was causin'
the van's sluggish acceleration....

And I can see the gasman smokin', his grin stretchin', then shrinkin'
in the rearview—O, I remember thinkin' I don't want to know
which side of the brain controls that! Which lobe is responsible
for queuin' the tasks in an emergency! Which nerve-
ending.

Before the War

Royal Beardtongue (Penstemon)

Here he chops a ripe cord in a whiteout by the treatment plant.
There she leans over a granite island high on the hill. She's kneading
the fair-trade rye with the clatter of daughters in the foreground.
With each blade strike, Jack pine tinctures the fog over the settling
pond & he draws the hard air a little deeper.

Meadow Rue (Thalictrum)

Sometimes a dayshift dream: She joins him on the spring-loaded
seat of a backhoe. She's left the kitchen unattended; the stove hisses,
flooding the house with gas. Her husband dozes while the wall-
paper curls from the fumes in the hours it takes to dig the trench.

Venus Thistle (Cirsium occidentale venustum)

Now he collects scrap, builds lean-tos for ghost soirees. He tells
time by the hum of arterials. Some nights, cross-legged by the tracks,
he pretends to pitch pennies to the trains. When the folding arms of
the crossing guard finally come down, she becomes nearly human again.

Fremont's Star Lily (Zigadenus fremontii)

Rain. Spring rain, like sheet metal and rolling pins. It wasn't always
this way. Once they held hands in the rain & wandered the town smelling
jasmine stamens by the bay. He'd pick brambleberries in jean cutoffs
while she plucked sea glass from the cobbles in a summer dress.

Creosote bush (Larrea tridentata)

With each spring's death summer comes a little harder. Record
heat leaves chalky ribbons ringing the sulky reservoir. Ruts like
lake wind ripples on a Wal-Mart tarmac, where an oversized cart
with a loose wheel steers her into oncoming traffic, and she nearly lets it.

California Poppy (Eschscholzia californica)

July 4: A procession of tubas. Children's laughter melting in
the trees. Veterans saluting one another under Main Street awnings
snapping in the wind. That was the last time she kissed him: July 4th
Dusk: They walked the briny shore, before the big show began.

Mochi Salvation

1.

This one does not care for nori but eats it to be polite. The
man she hopes to marry does not ask if she wants more sake
before emptying the warm vessel into his cup. They've draped
matching bomber jackets over the backrests of the bar chairs.
She clicks the heels of her knee-high boots as he mumbles
something about a forthcoming fly-fishing trip. At forty-three,
he's having a midlife brain-freeze. She no longer wants to hike
and has given up Pilates. She has recently passed a threshold.

2.

In the booth opposite the couple in exile, another woman
sobs into her menu. Her husband has taken a job in another
state. He says it's temporary, insists it beats the military and
they should be grateful for a job, any job… Meanwhile, a
boy and a girl of her likeness, with sandy blond hair and
witch hazel eyes, in unison, ask for more of the shrimp rolls.
At times, she can be the strongest person in the world—*a
rock star*—her coworkers at the Public Employees Retirement
System regional headquarters tell her. Though this is not one
of those moments.

3.

Behind fogged glass, a man's face is flushed with the excitement
that must come from cutting through line-caught fish. In the
gilded mirror, sumo wrestlers on a flat screen embrace in a full-
body kiss. She thinks of her husband alone in a diner west of
Thermopolis. A woman with a dragon tattoo on her chest and
a silver stud in her lip leans over his shoulder. When the
waitress, an androgynous waif, comes closer, the children are no
longer bickering but eating the last of the veggie tempura,
rocking contently back and forth in the booth. Now they ask if
they can order the mango and coconut mochi.

Three Moments of Silence

Here is the toddler learning to walk

This is the day she packs for college

Here is the way you give her away
    as though she were yours to give.

III. Song of the California Wildfire

"*There were people who did not listen.
There were people who got critically injured
because they did not listen.
Our hearts are heavy.*"

ARNOLD SCHWARZENEGGER, Governor of California,
on the Angeles National Forest Wildfire, 2009

Pastoral

Not arson, but a boy & a girl playing with matches
in the oat grass; a cherry bomb his big brother gave him,
without instructions.

Placer County Roadside Marker

Here is the Goth whose father sleeps
around. She is the Purple Heart he keeps
on the mantel. She's packed the camo
duffle, stuffed it in the blue Beetle she stole
from her ex's shop. She punches it with
the top down. Hwy 49 wends south
through scrub oak like a black snake
or a garter snug on the leg of the Mother
Lode: Gold Country. Peach Blossom
Ghosts of Crocker's Chinese Railroad
men. She can't get away fast enough
She longs for the scent of bull pines slung
among the swayback hills of Calaveras
County. Angel's Camp. Sweet gin from
a still. Scruff of a boy's chin on her lap
Promise of a little lakeside tryst. She's
famished when she arrives on his door-
step. He hands her a fistful of yellow
asters, runs a hot bath with lavender salts
and feeds her a rib eye steak. His single-
wide is homey and she's happy here. The
floozies and the whiskey fits, the night
terrors, and the strange calls for bail
all fade like a crass mural on the bar's
south wall. She'll never fall in love
again, she tells him in the dream. She'll
never return to That Devil! She'll
sleep here forever, if that's what it takes,
turning under a canopy of aspens
buried in amethyst lupines.

Farallones (Gulls In The Absence of Stars)

Prologue: g-e-l... g-l-e... g-a-l... g-u-l-l?

ma'am you'll have to bear with me,
our circuits are overloaded. ma'am

i have no messages no record of his
checking-in. search-n-rescue is stuck

in port and the storm has scuttled
our server... how do you spell that,

again?

1.
we are the deckhands with ghost faces
our wives have gone mad on the cape

cormorants set gold hooks into our palms
and heels and tug like rodeo clowns

mergansers cast their silver net down
and let the wind cinch it...

gulls cry in the distance; they are innocent
and hungry

2.
gulls have no religion no deity
but believe in a higher disorder:

heaven's bad hand

3.
messengers of salt and soot in the storm, gulls

shift moods like white churches
in the rain

they know the deeper pain
in the margins

4.
gulls: crows in sheep's clothing
sheared by the sea

5.

gulls do not scavenge your Christmas
wishes

no gull mourns the tinseled fir
in the airy dumpster

or the flocked pine on fire
in the fifty-gallon drum

6.

when we were young
we played in the waves

& thought it good luck
when a gull would shit on us—

the world was full of
potential

7.
drifting past the drilling rig
we cheer

gulls shitting on yellow
hardhats—

we listen for the engineers'
cursing

which reminds us we are all
human we are all

hungry

8.
she wanted to take him home
make him her suitor

snuggle in his wing of down
& dream

he would tell her of the greatest
herring runs in the world

a sea thick with silver sequins
from the gulls thrashing them apart

but her father, a crabber at heart,
would have none of it—

so a landlocked maiden she remained
& grew gills in her sleep

through slits in her neck
on a yellow barbed pillow

9.
first an airmail bride
bearing gifts

then a wrecking crew

soon multiples of fifty descend,
a low cloud over your city

they pluck municipal pigeons
& *kids' meals* from the local landfill—

at slack-tide a stale sea-smell
permeates your cab

the freeway at a standstill
gulls nowhere in sight

10.
90 degrees in the valley
crows on the tarmac

barking at gulls—
the gulls laugh, tie loops

set treble hooks
in the trees

11.
some gulls are related
to bees

daubs of blood
on yellow beaks

mark the rape

12.
eclipsed sunsets are for lovers
of tragedy

gulls know the routine
& practice it

in their sleep

13.
here the speckled gull
cocks

his head,
watches the deck-

hand suture himself

while a white gull
whispers

in his wife's ear
she dreams

crushed petals, a girl
dancing

the shore-break—

gulls run
interference

for the sharks
smell her longing

for father
from the other side of

the reef

From *The Inferno*

When the red-eye triple trailer
broke through the Jersey barrier
a few of us rubbernecked long
enough to see the man climb
from the collapsed sleeper
behind the smashed-in cab...

You were there that night
I saw you creeping along
the shoulder trying not to
stare. But you couldn't help
yourself. I saw you licking your
palms, wiping them on your jeans.

Song of the California Wildfire 80% Contained

"While thousands fled, two people who tried to ride out the firestorm in a backyard hot tub were burned."
–LOS ANGELES COUNTY SHERIFF, August 2009

Once they were like flames
licking barnwood

They stole little kisses
in the break room

& flew to Modesto on
questionable business—

They did this for
years, some say—

Then a rumor, a little
evidence under the dash

A lingerie ad
left on the fax tray...

They couldn't outrun
their own flames

Now nothing
but cinders remain:

drab dabs of ash
on their lips

& the future

Advance Directive

He keeps writing I already
miss you

on all his checks.
He's making a list of things

he will never do again.
It begins with alpine skiing

and ends at bowling.
He's stuck in a drift, calls it

Splitting Kindling
and it's a lot harder than

it looks. He's preparing for
a terminal illness

brought on by lead shot
residue and chromium in the

groundwater. He's in training
for brain cancer

because you can never be
too prepared.

Elegy for Silicon Valley

When everyone is asleep
and she's feeling small

in the mute country
of foreclosed homes

she'll walk out
onto the plastic decking

of the undersized porch
and ask questions, like:

What are moths good for? and
Do they converse with the last owls? and

If so, what conspiracies do they tap-out
on the white Halogenas

in their odd Braille?

He's Got Mail

One of his contacts died
four months ago
and no one knows how
to update her profile.

For the first month he felt
like barfing into a Dixie cup
then the feeling faded
on receiving an e-vite.

He's multitasking
his procrastination now
The yellow flower on his
screensaver

is missing a pixel
and he's trying to fix it
with rubber cement—

This is the age we live in.

After Leaving You In Santa Monica

He is half-here in the hollow
of his rural commute

Sunday lingers into the work-
week like a feral cat

and he fumbles with the Blue-
tooth trying to reach you

Your scent on his collar,
jasmine, distracts—

You nearly overtake the smell
of truck brakes burning.

Moments Before Loma Prieta

7.1 earthquake, October 17, 1989

Here the Pajaro nuzzles riprap
and gathers trash below a row of
idling semis, where redeye triple
trailer drivers listen to Scott Turrow
on tape, and a man-boy with a mad face

Sits cross-legged with his girl.
She's wrapped in burlap and a pink
quilt, hunkered in the phosphorescence
under restroom eave. A wool cap
hides her eyes, though her hands

Appear delicate. Their life might be
old weather. You may know each other
from the seventh-grade, where he sat
next to you diagramming pipe bombs.
You were almost best friends,

but she kept glancing at him from the hall.
Now he fiddles with an empty leash, soothes
the black lab Dad would never let him have,
while rocking a makeshift sign that pleads:

HELP / NEED MONEY / GAS / FOOD
A PLACE TO STAY / GOD BLESS...

Her brass nose ring:
It winks at you.

The Contortionist of Pacific Palisades

He was good at getting it up. She knew many ways
But in this case there was only one. She had a flat
back and great sense of balance. He hardly had to
exert himself. Their only task to guide her slender
legs over a slick white banister. He made sure she
cleared the chandelier, before turning the corner
She had the straightest teeth. She came perfectly
tuned.

Santa Cruz Carney Girl

I am not a stereotype
I do not even own a stereo!
My iPod is stuck on public radio
It replays the podcast on women's
liberation, over and over; I can't quite

Figure it out—I think I might be a lesbian
Does any of this make sense?
I'd like your opinion. Come here
before they open the gates,
before the freaks flood the place

With their desperate wives
and overweight children—
Come! before I become
invisible again, part of the
machinery.

R is Not for Rollercoaster

Hello, my name is Ralph
My road ends at the beach
It is a boardwalk with no
body-builders

At the end of the walk
I stop & look up: A prop
plane muffled by the heat
of our hell has stalled

One hundred five degrees
the clock keeps dripping…
I take off my shirt and get
in line. I am the fisherman

Whose trawler they re-
possessed. Now I grease axles
and retighten bolts
on the cogs of the *Holy Oyster*

Here cars climb
above and below
the spot
where my wrench rests

I reach for it
and my stomach groans,
longing for the chilidog
that eludes me…

Now the sun rises over the derricks,
smug & devilish, and the twinge
in my knee rears like a lion,
and all goes silent:

A cool little wind off the Pacific
spins and dies over the desert
never reaching me—
I raise my arm and sniff:

This could be the end of the world
Yet I can't help wondering
whether that girl
restocking the snack shack is smiling
and whether her name begins with

R.

Santa Fe, Fiesta

September 11, 2011

1.

One gnaws a roasted pork leg, ropes
    my stare
from across the lawn

    of the town square. Full-bodied
and brown,

    she's beautiful.

2.

Her sister, at least
    eight years younger,
    squats,

applies tangerine
    lip-
gloss,
    tucks
her left

    bosom
back
    inside

the white vee-
    neck
tee.

3.

   I am standing in the shade
of a burnt-orange

      garden wall
where Georgia

      O'Keeffe's ghost
dabs yellow
         brush-
strokes

      from moist
mouths
      of freshly-cut

pinion
      blossoms.

4.

   I wish I were
born
      in New Mexico

in the shadow
      of the Sangre
de Cristo;

      half-Pueblo,
half-Chicano,
      I could be

happy here.

5.

When two boys meet
    on the streets of
Santa Fe
    it is a mute

drum-beat:
part–
    war chant
part–

    mariachi.

6.

Here are the ripped
    shoulders of
brothers

    with arched
backs,
    whose forearms

flex,
    and whose swagger
of toothy grins,
    with fist-pumps to boot,

    make a white
like me

    so jealous.

7.

They meet
    at dusk
to Claps!
    of fists;
elbows knock
    knuckles

to unfold
    fingers,
which like cocks'
    tail-feathers
fan-out

    and flutter
then duck
    then veer
to clasp
    and dive
like hawks
    embraced
in a familial
    hand-

shake—

8.

I saw and heard the racket
    commence
across the square
    when one muttered
"Hey Brother"
    amidst the laughter
and polka
    of Fiesta—

9.

At first, the men converged
    like slow arrows;
but they met
    in a quick clutch
of:
    I love ya, Bro'!s

which echoed against
    the orange
stucco
    of a minimart;

    then brushed the bricks
of the Museum
    of Modern Art;

then refracted

    and were absorbed
by the four-hundred
    year-old timbers of
a conquistador's
    palace.

10.

When the women finally turned
    and grinned,
having watched the dance
    of full-grown boys
long enough,

the chest-shoves must have meant
    the men would not fight,
and the women could return to
    pantomiming

the same old rumors
    and refrains
against the ash-white
    stones
of the federal
    courthouse

as a riot
    of Sunday nightfall
church bells
    signaled the end
of another year's

Fiesta.

IV. Drawbridge

*In the tall grass, the town's broken roofs sag
like swaybacked horses out to pasture.
Endangered San Joaquin kit foxes emerge
from culverts, and burrowing owls glide
beneath power lines. In every direction,
commercial parks shimmer like mirages.*

NICK NEELY
High Country News, Dec. 2010

Drawbridge

Barn's burnt down—
now
I can see the moon.

    MIZUTA MASAHIDE

What I believe is, when we leave this world
we become UFOs, and when we collide in that state
inexplicable things happen here on Earth

Once when I was eight, my mother and father saw an alien
ship hover over Los Altos. It was late. An odd pall
permeated the guts of our trailer. My father shook me

awake and pulled me into the overhead sleeper
where my mother lived most of that year. She half-
knelt on scabbed elbows and pointed toward

an odd bulge in the altostratus, where a second moon,
then a third, pulsed and converged, as the real moon,
·a stepchild, hunkered in a notch to east.

The crescent had turned away from the stars
as an animal does before it dies, and it moaned
into a purple vase—

I remember being hungry that year. We burned
slash, poached deer, and siphoned gasoline to survive;
but we were royalty that night, when aliens,

like moths, were drawn to our trailer…
Though as quickly as they appeared, the lights stuttered
and slid across the frets of the bay's rim

like a giant roulette wheel, off-kilter,
or a military jet maneuver—They disappeared
through a pinhole in the night.

Report from The New Common Era

In the beginning, the weather was self-effacing
& stubborn. The globe went into a funk. Some
lucky ones found arable land in the unlikeliest
places. The last of the freshwater lakes made
excellent farms.

Then dust blew over us like a cape
& hovered for three thousand years. Entire
tribes disappeared while we waited.
The consumers & adulterers were the first
to go; we gave them proper burials...

We learned to digest saltgrass, lived on
reverse osmosis—Prayer was a luxury—
Then skeletons returned in a flourish
to save us. In the beginning, our skeletons
did all the work.

Out Here

after Ursula Le Guin's "Out Here"

A coyote's frozen in perpetual leap-the-razor-
wire pose

You cannot own a desert but hard water will lease you

You fishtail off-road the sky snares you with its
laugh

You conjure antelope hoofs strike alkali flats. Like
matchsticks

they kick-up the brine shrimp, & you lick
the bitter crust

You heard there is a diner but the herd has wandered

Steens means laughter while longing for a steak

When a fake creek swells you overcorrect

Three crows make a raven repairing the road. Nine
ripen a heron loose from the reeds

                              But a heron here
is a tame pterodactyl, a living fossil—

The desert is not an island, but an inland sea

Eclipse Over Alturas

1.

winter here feels like her
jawbone

when we'd kiss against
the split–rail…

the bedspread always reeked
of juniper

2.

once we hid and kissed;
then sleep interrupted the dream

& the fantasy went
monochrome…

this is what it was like,
the first hot nights

turning over
to morning with you

Chromium Tahoe

after Lake Tahoe

1.

here we dive from a granite boulder into the frigid womb
then rise like krill to the surface

we can't help kicking harder than necessary
dangerous business in forty-degree water

sixteen hundred feet below our pale toes
something lurking

our heartbeats throbbing like the round
gears of the earth's cartilage

2.

after years of drought record snowfall defies the almanac
the body of the lake feels nostalgic

kisses touching down & the storm singing through the night
like the spaces between songs on my dusty vinyl records

i keep lifting the needle, replaying my favorites

3.

yes, pines know the smell of their own kind
burning

even under the trestles of windy ridges
like anemones

they feel blindly, smoke writhing,
they read it like braille

4.

now i linger below grade listening for fissures
in the cool cellar that is my sickness

through a portal called spring, snowmelt torques
the birches like a wet ratchet

when winter blanket melts, the basement oozes
a wet wool smell, a girlish tincture

then earth thaws, shifts imperceptibly,
& mountains rise, pulling apart roads, cables, gas lines…

meanwhile, high up in the aspen chorus
of my childhood, power poles lean and sing

Request for Proposals (RFP)

Courtesy of the State of California

Project Number: 202048   *come closer small mammal*
Name: Recovery of Giant Garter Snake Habitat   *inhabitant of gray cubicle*
Agency: State of California; Schedule: TBD   *my brood of thirty grows hungry*

Terms: Lump Sum   *when aquifers slump*
Not to Exceed   *& spring floods disappear*
No Stimulus Funding   *in dusty cavities*

Deadline: *watch us mutate*
Rolling   *in your long thin shadow…*

\#   ξ

★★★Update★★★   ★★★*hurry now*★★★

Project Awarded To: *the ocean*
Cancelled   *is rising*

\#

Entering the Desert *

1.

they prayed and laughed   the june sky rocketed over
and were full of one another latent heat made his palms ache
in the calming wake   her feet burned blue
of evening's fire...   the air tinctured with sage...

2.

arriving with a smile   dusk on the hills' ruddy silhouette
and a kiss   swept the lakebed bare
and a hope   blushed the east buttes red
for further exploration... the moon's contours: the warm crevices...

3.

in dawn's first beams   she gave no refrain
dancing in the darkness   they staved the dawn
he basked in her   she made his blood roil
warm privileges...   they shared desert confections

4.

with the taste of the moon   he descended the tamarisk
filling his senses   burning like a hawk's eyes
complete and still... before a kill

just touching the note that sang   she was birdsong in the willows
in the rising light... oh,   how they would learn
how the day sounds!   how all love must run aground!

* "Entering the Desert" is a collaboration with Kristin Isgett

Barstow

Put on bra. Open door
for pizza guy. Sign receipt.
Close door. Take off bra.

K. ISGETT "Dateless Saturday Night"

He awoke in a dry riverbed
with a mouthful of silt,
blue marker in his hand...

Once he'd rise with the men
in yellow hardhats,
ride D-9 cats,

burn slash & burl
by day, turn the dawn
sky LA-orange—

He's a good worker, they'd say;
they trusted him with pine stakes
& pink ribbons

His traverses were faultless;
they called him a
transit wizard

But at dusk, when the others
would turn away, he'd lean over
like a cripple

& take a long, hard drag
on that blue marker,
just missing her.

Actuary Table

Look into your soup
and divide by three

Fire Poker

The dog that lives in a house
is the broken dog

The man who dwells in the wood
howls at the dog-eared moon

The house that holds the dog's bowl
is a house of iron & stone

No man is ever home
in a dog house—

But a woman, a real woman,
stays home

With a broken dog,
a man who howls at the moon

When she stokes the fire, that cold
fire grows

And the children know, as children
always know,

who's master

Big Bang

Galileo was a pious heretic
Hubble had an eye of onyx

Some things in the world
have not already happened

There is no such thing as light
poetry—A shaft of darkness
runs through everything—

Einstein lived a double-life
as a cantor, whose elegies

can be heard forever, ringing
through the cosmos

Heaven of the Moment

After John Morrison's "Heaven of the Moment"

She scared herself on her horse today,
loping over the mole-pocked paddock
at the Lone Star Ranch. First day
of dry weather in months. The sky,
through the sycamore branches, was
a stern vole. A black lab frolicked
on the hill. The air bristled with velocity

Cars pulled over just to watch her
She was that beautiful moving across
the deep green field on a chestnut horse
Though she knew from his breathing,
something wasn't right. The lab was really
a wolf on the hill. The tourists had become

Iron figurines cast against the witch's wood
His gait was a drumbeat, a human femur
on an elk skin bodhran. She grabbed a hand-
ful of mane and closed her eyes. Mother
looking on...The horse huffing glue,
lunging for an imaginary heaven

Snow Descending on Oakland

I never wanted to go
I didn't want it to end

Wind on wild poppies
still excites me

A condor off-leash
at Tilden Park—

Please don't start—
I never wanted to leave

Just let me breathe
for a moment,

the crushed leaves
of the Bay Laurel

the Live Oak
& the Blue Gum

Eucalyptus;
just for a minute,

before I slip uphill
on these skis of corkwood

Muse on Mount Hood

The language of landscape is mute and immaculate
CHARLES WRIGHT

Dear youngest daughter, fellow poet
I think of you under your sheets hiding
a storm of your own making

building outside your window. On wings
of lenticulars, like bats, dreams tug
our tents, yours & mine, from afar…

We are geologists; we fill our pockets
with carnelian agates & less beautiful
specimens: clam shells

split & riddled by sea lice; false-fossils
bits of iron slag we haul in T-shirt
rucksacks from the shoreline…

We keep these things close like talismans
to ward-off nightmares & stranger
premonitions… We care for them

like brittle birds, the way I care for these
words, little glass origami I carry
down the mountain
to tell you

someday

Off-Ramp

Sylvan Exit, back of
the Chevron, his wife runs
the operation. Greets us
from a portal called

Chinatown. With mortar
& pestle she crumbles
Herbs. Claws. Dried
Innards. Fills paper

Bags... I smell vats
of Turtles. Gin-
seng. HVAC clanging...
We had to rebuild her

Immune system
would try anything:
Acupuncture. Wild-
flowers. It's all about

The blood, they say...
He sticks one right
in her bridge; though
she does bleed

She does not tremble...
They send us away
with a thimble:
$15 worth of herbs...

Two weeks later, she's
off steroids. Feeling
nimble. No more
migraine. No more tingle

For the first time in years,
our storm feels right—
This is Portland,
where Doug firs sway
above the freeway roar!

Thousands Flee California Wildflowers is SCOT SIEGEL's second full-length poetry collection. His other volumes include *Some Weather, Untitled Country*, and *Skeleton Says*. Siegel's poems are anthologized in the *Aesthetica Creative Works Annual* (UK), *Open Spaces: Voices from the Northwest* (Seattle: University of Washington Press, 2011), *Dogs Singing: A Tribute Anthology* (County Clare, Ireland: Salmon Poetry 2010), and *Before We Have Nowhere to Stand* (Sandpoint, ID: Lost Horse Press 2012), among others. He has been awarded a residency from Playa, and has received awards and commendations from A*esthetica Magazine, Nimrod International*, and the *Oregon Poetry Association*. He is a member of the Squaw Valley Community of Writers and edits the online poetry journal *Untitled Country Review*. More information is available at Red Room: www.redroom.com/author/scot-siegel/